Marricdale Productions in association
with Neil McPherson for the Finborou

The world premiere

CHECKPOINT CHANA

by Jeff Page

FINBOROUGH | THEATRE

First performed at the Finborough Theatre as a staged reading
as part of *Vibrant 2017 – A Festival of Finborough Playwrights*:
Thursday, 12 October 2017.

First performance at the Finborough Theatre: Sunday, 4 March 2018.

CHECKPOINT CHANA

by Jeff Page

Cast in order of speaking

Tamsin	**Ulrika Krishnamurti**
Bev	**Geraldine Somerville**
David	**Matt Mella**
Michael	**Nathaniel Wade**

The action takes place in a North London flat and an Arts Centre in Camden. The present.

The performance lasts approximately seventy-five minutes.

There will be no interval.

Director	**Manuel Bau**
Designer	**Daisy Blower**
Lighting Designer	**Jamie Platt**
Sound Designer	**Simon Arrowsmith**
Stage Manager	**Xanthe Goode**
Producer	**Genevieve Burns**

Our patrons are respectfully reminded that, in this intimate theatre, any noise such as rustling programmes, talking or the ringing of mobile phones may distract the actors and your fellow audience-members.

We regret there is no admittance or re-admittance to the auditorium whilst the performance is in progress.

Checkpoint Chana is performed in repertoire and on the set of *Returning to Haifa*, designed by Rosie Elnile, with lighting design by Joshua Gadsby, which plays Tuesday to Saturday evenings, and Saturday and Sunday matinees, until 24 March 2018.

Ulrika Krishnamurti | Tamsin
Trained at Guildford School of
Acting and Act One Studios in
Chicago.

Theatre includes *Made in India*
for which she was nominated for
an OffWestEnd Award for Best
Female in a Play (Soho Theatre,
Belgrade Theatre, Coventry,
and National Tour), *Pink Sari
Revolution* (The Curve, Leicester,
Belgrade Theatre, Coventry,
and West Yorkshire Playhouse),
Sanguine Night (RADA Festival),
Commencing (Tristan Bates
Theatre) and *Twelve* (Kali
Theatre).

Film includes *The Anushree
Experiments*, *London Paris New
York* and *Rockford*.

Matt Mella | David
Trained at the Royal Central
School of Speech and Drama.

Theatre includes *The Merry Wives
of Windsor* (Theatre N16), *The
Doctor in Spite of Himself* (Drayton
Arms Theatre), *In the Dead of the
Night* (Landor Theatre), *Grease,
Company, Edmond, Hamlet* and
Antigone (Royal Central School of
Speech and Drama).

Film includes *Par for the Course.*
Voiceover includes *The World's
End, Prisoners* and *Goosebumps.*

Geraldine Somerville | Bev
Trained at the Guildhall School of
Music and Drama.

Theatre includes *Power,
Remember This* and *Blue
Remembered Hills* (National
Theatre), *I Am Yours, The
Treatment, 3 Birds Alighting on
a Field* and *A Jamaican Airman
Foresees His Death* (Royal
Court Theatre), *Yerma* (New Vic,
Bristol), *More Than One Antoinette*
(The Young Vic), *Epsom Downs*
and *Romeo and Juliet* (Bristol
Old Vic), *Lady Audrey's Secret*
(Lyric Theatre, Hammersmith),
The Glass Menagerie for which
she was nominated for the
Manchester Evening News Award
for Best Actress (Royal Exchange
Theatre, Manchester), *Serenading
Louise* (Donmar Warehouse and
National Tour) and *A Doll's House*
(Birmingham Rep).

Film includes *Harry Potter and the
Chamber of Secrets, Harry Potter
and the Philosopher's Stone, Harry
Potter and the Goblet of Fire,
Harry Potter and the Order of the
Phoenix, Harry Potter and the Half-
Blood Prince, Harry Potter and
the Deathly Hallows Part 1, Harry
Potter and the Deathly Hallows
Part 2, Goodbye Christopher
Robin, The Hippopotamus, Kids
in Love, The Riot Club, Grace of*

Monaco, Automata, My Week with Marilyn, Sixty Six, Gosford Park, Rough Auntie, Jilting Joe, True Blue, Haunted, A Business Affair, Close My Eyes, Augustine and *Bathing Elizabeth*.

Television includes *Cracker* for which she was nominated for a BAFTA TV Award for Best Actress, *The Children, Daphne, The Inspector Lynley Mysteries, Jericho, Murder in Mind, The Safe House, New Tricks, Silent Witness, Quirke, Inspector George Gently, Survivors, Heaven on Earth, Daylight Robbery, The Aristocrats, Heaven on Earth, After Miss Julie, The Deep Blue Sea, Romeo and Juliet, Poirot, Casualty* and *The Black Velvet Gown*.

Forthcoming productions include Netflix and Channel 4's new drama *Kiss Me First*.

Nathaniel Wade | Michael
Trained with the National Youth Theatre Rep Company.

Theatre includes *Cinderella* (Lyric Theatre, Hammersmith), *DNA, Pigeon English* and *Romeo and Juliet* (Ambassadors Theatre) and *Boys* (The Vaults).

Jeff Page | Playwright
Jeff Page is a writer and voluntary sector worker. He is a graduate of the John Burgess playwriting course at the Nuffield Theatre, Southampton. Plays include *Attack of the A&E Zombies* (Descent Theatre and Irlam Festival Fringe).

Manuel Bau | Director
Productions at the Finborough Theatre include the staged reading of *Checkpoint Chana* as part of *Vibrant 2017 – A Festival of Finborough Playwrights*.

Trained at the London Film Academy and Lincoln Center, New York, after having graduated in Theatre Directing in Venice.

Direction includes *Questions of Terrorism and Repression* (Lion and Unicorn Theatre), *A Feyre Tale* (The Space, Edinburgh Festival), *The Man with The Flower in His Mouth* (Christ Church College, Oxford), *How Does That Make You Feel?* (Lion and Unicorn Theatre), *Soft the Moon Rose* (Etcetera Theatre), *The White Room* (Courtyard Theatre) and *Girls Just Want to Have Fun-Damental Human Rights, Girl of My Dreams* and *The Lottery* (Theatre503 and Southwark Playhouse).

Associate Direction includes *Le Grand Mort* (Trafalgar Studios), *How to Succeed in Business Without Really Trying* (Royal Festival Hall) and *Allegro* (Southwark Playhouse).

Manuel was recently Language Consultant on *Do I Hear a Waltz?* (Encores at New York City Center) and Director on Attachment on *Porgy and Bess* (Open Air Theatre, Regent's Park).

Daisy Blower | Designer

Productions at the Finborough Theatre include *Cyril's Success.*

Theatre includes *A Peril of the Sea* (Lakeside Theatre and Bloomsbury Theatre), *A Midsummer Night's Dream* (Orange Tree Theatre, Richmond), *Third Wheel* and *Predrinks/Afterparty* (Underbelly, Edinburgh Festival), *The Big Meal* and *Accidental Death of an Anarchist* (Alma Tavern, Bristol) and *Vernon God Little* (Winston Theatre, Bristol).

Associate and Assistant work includes *The Dog Beneath the Skin* (Jermyn Street Theatre), *A Pacifist's Guide to the War on Cancer* (Everyman Theatre, Liverpool, and National Tour), *Mrs Orwell* (Old Red Lion Theatre), *The Secret Theatre* (Shakespeare's Globe) and *Bat Out of Hell* (London Coliseum).

She was also Front of House Designer on *The Grinning Man* (Trafalgar Studios).

Jamie Platt | Lighting Design

Productions at the Finborough Theatre include *Quaint Honour*, *P'yongyang*, *We Know Where You Live* and *Chicken Dust.*

Trained at the Royal Welsh College of Music and Drama. He was nominated for Best Lighting Design OffWestEnd Awards in 2015 and 2016, and awarded the Association of Lighting Designer's ETC Award and the Royal Welsh College of Music and Drama Carne Prize in 2013.

Theatre includes *Yous Two* (Hampstead Theatre), *Le Grand Mort* (Trafalgar Studios), *To Dream Again* (Clwyd Theatre Cymru and Polka Theatre), *The Moor*, *Where Do Little Birds Go?* (Old Red Lion Theatre), *Beast, Klippies* (Southwark Playhouse), *Pattern Recognition* (Platform Theatre and World Tour), *Screwed*, *Grey Man* (Theatre503), *The Trap* (Omnibus Theatre), *The Wonderful World of Dissocia* (Embassy Theatre), *Snow White*, *He Shoots! He Scores!*, *B*tches Ahoy!* and *Beauty on the Piste* (Above The Stag Theatre), *Constellations* (Théâtre Municipal de Fontainebleau), *YOU* and *Mr. Incredible* (The Vaults), *House of America* (Brockley Jack Studio Theatre), *And Now: The World!* (Derby Theatre and National Tour), *Make/Believe* (Victoria and Albert Museum), *Ring the Changes+* (Southbank Centre and National Tour), *Mahmud íle Yezida*, *BOY*, *Misbehaving*, *The Intruder*, *Bald Prima Donna* and *The Red Helicopter* (Arcola Theatre), *The Eulogy of Toby Peach* (Criterion Theatre and National Tour), *Closer to Heaven* (Union Theatre), *My Land's Shore* (Theatr Soar, Merthyr Tydfil) and *110 In The Shade* (Rose and Crown Theatre).

Associate Lighting Design includes *Ink* (Duke of York's Theatre) for Neil Austin, *Depart* (National Tour), *The Grit in the Oyster* (Sadler's Wells and International Tour), *The Measures Taken* and *All That Is Solid Melts Into Air* (Royal Opera House, Covent Garden and International Tour) and *Our Big Land* (New Wolsey Theatre, Ipswich, and National Tour) all for Lee Curran.

Simon Arrowsmith | Sound Design
Graduated from Manchester Metropolitan University with a First-Class BA Hons and Masters in Contemporary Arts. His performance work has been selected for festivals and showcases including Greenroom, Manchester, Nottingham Live Arts Festival, London's ICA, and as part of the National Review of Live Art.

Composition includes *The View from Nowhere* (Park Theatre), *Something Something Lazarus* (King's Head Theatre), *April in Paris* (English Theatre of Hamburg) and *Two Gentlemen of Verona* (German Tour).

He also produces music for films and games. His most recent project is *The Monarch Papers*, an interactive year-long story from New York author C J Bernstein.

Genevieve Burns | Producer
Productions at the Finborough Theatre include Assistant Producer on *Into the Numbers* and *Vibrant 2017 – A Festival of Finborough Playwrights*.

Theatre includes *Queens of Sheba* (Camden People's Theatre), *The Princes' Quest* (C Venues, Edinburgh), *Spamalot* (Gala Theatre, Durham), *Oliver Twist* (Durham Markets), *Swallow* and *Ordinary Days* (National Student Drama Festival, Hull), *Kiss Me, Kate* (National Student Drama Festival, Scarborough).

She is currently a General Management Intern at Selladoor Worldwide.

Production Acknowledgements
Production Photography | **Samuel Kirkman**
Image Design | **Isabella Giorgio**
Casting Director | **Aurora Causin**
Casting Assistant | **Tabitha Hayward**

Checkpoint Chana has been generously funded by the Unity Theatre Trust who have a long history of bringing politically-relevant theatre to fruition.

Thanks to Olivia Carney, Jennie Church, Richard Hand, Gina Hills, Anne Marcuson, Sophie Morgan-Price, Tim O'Hara, and Brett M. Rhyne.

FINBOROUGH | THEATRE

The Finborough Theatre's building – including both the Finborough Arms pub and the Finborough Theatre – celebrates its 150th birthday in 2018.

Opened in 1868, the building was designed by one of the leading architects of his day, George Godwin (1813-1888) who was also the editor of the architectural magazine *The Builder* (which is still published today), and a sometime playwright. He is buried in nearby Brompton Cemetery.

The Finborough Arms was one of five public houses originally constructed as part of the Redcliffe Estate – and one of only three that still survive as pubs today.

One of the Finborough Arms' most regular customers was sanitary pioneer Thomas Crapper (1836-1910) who would would regularly begin his working day in the Finborough Arms with a bottle of champagne. His daughter, Minnie, married Ernest Finch (who was born in the flat above the theatre) of the Finch family who owned and managed the building from its opening in 1868 until the early 1930s.

The building had a near-miss during the Blitz of 1940-41 when a high explosive bomb destroyed the houses just across the street.

FINBOROUGH | THEATRE

VIBRANT **NEW WRITING** | UNIQUE **REDISCOVERIES**

"Probably the most influential fringe theatre in the world."
Time Out

"Under Neil McPherson, possibly the most unsung of all major artistic directors in Britain, the Finborough has continued to plough a fertile path of new plays and rare revivals that gives it an influence disproportionate to its tiny 50-seat size."
Mark Shenton, *The Stage* 2017

"The tiny but mighty Finborough…one of the best batting averages of any London company"
Ben Brantley, *The New York Times*

Founded in 1980 on the first floor of the building (which was previously been a restaurant, a Masonic Lodge, and a billiards hall), the multi-award-winning Finborough Theatre presents plays and music theatre, concentrated exclusively on vibrant new writing and unique rediscoveries from the 19th and 20th centuries.

Our programme is unique – we never present work that has been seen anywhere in London during the last 25 years.

Do visit us our website to find out more about us, or follow us on Facebook, Twitter, Instagram, Tumblr and YouTube.

For more on the history of the building and the local area, and for full information on the Finborough Theatre's work, visit our website at **www.finboroughtheatre.co.uk**

Mailing
Email admin@finboroughtheatre.co.uk or give your details to our
Box Office staff to join our free email list.

Feedback
We welcome your comments, complaints and suggestions.
Write to Finborough Theatre, 118 Finborough Road, London SW10 9ED
or email us at admin@finboroughtheatre.co.uk

Playscripts
Many of the Finborough Theatre's plays have been published and are
on sale from our website.

On Social Media

 www.facebook.com/FinboroughTheatre

 www.twitter.com/finborough

 finboroughtheatre.tumblr.com

 www.instagram.com/finboroughtheatre

 www.youtube.com/user/finboroughtheatre

Friends
The Finborough Theatre is a registered charity. We receive no public
funding, and rely solely on the support of our audiences. Please do
consider supporting us by becoming a member of our Friends of the
Finborough Theatre scheme. There are four categories of Friends,
each offering a wide range of benefits.

Richard Tauber Friends – David and Melanie Alpers. J. D. Anderson.
Mark Bentley. Kate Beswick. Simon Bolland. James Carroll. Deirdre
Feehan. N. and D. Goldring. Loyd Grossman. Paul Guinery. David Harrison.
Mary Hickson. Richard Jackson. Paul and Lindsay Kennedy. Martin
and Wendy Kramer. John Lawson. Kathryn McDowall. Ghazell Mitchell.
Guislaine Vincent Morland. Carol Rayman. Barry Serjent. Brian Smith.
Lavinia Webb. Sandra Yarwood.

Lionel Monckton Friends – Philip G Hooker.

William Terriss Friends – Stuart Ffoulkes. Alan Godfrey. Ros Haigh.
Melanie Johnson. Leo and Janet Liebster.

Smoking is not permitted in the auditorium and the use of cameras and recording equipment is strictly prohibited.

In accordance with the requirements of the Royal Borough of Kensington and Chelsea:
1. The public may leave at the end of the performance by all doors and such doors must at that time be kept open.

2. All gangways, corridors, staircases and external passageways intended for exit shall be left entirely free from obstruction whether permanent or temporary.

3. Persons shall not be permitted to stand or sit in any of the gangways intercepting the seating or to sit in any of the other gangways.

The Finborough Theatre is licensed by the Royal Borough of Kensington and Chelsea to The Steam Industry, a registered charity and a company limited by guarantee. Registered in England and Wales no. 3448268. Registered Charity no. 1071304. Registered Office: 118 Finborough Road, London SW10 9ED.

The Steam Industry was founded by Phil Willmott in 1992. It comprises two strands to its work: the Finborough Theatre (under Artistic Director Neil McPherson); and The Phil Willmott Company (under Artistic Director Phil Willmott) which presents productions throughout London as well as annually at the Finborough Theatre.

Jeff Page

CHECKPOINT CHANA

OBERON BOOKS
LONDON

WWW.OBERONBOOKS.COM

First published in 2018 by Oberon Books Ltd
521 Caledonian Road, London N7 9RH
Tel: +44 (0) 20 7607 3637 / Fax: +44 (0) 20 7607 3629
e-mail: info@oberonbooks.com
www.oberonbooks.com

A catalogue record for this book is available from the British
Library.

PB ISBN: 9781786824554
E ISBN: 9781786824561

Cover design by Isabella Giorgio

Printed and bound by 4EDGE Limited, Hockley, Essex, UK.
eBook conversion by CPI Group (UK) Ltd, Croydon, CR0 4YY.

Visit www.oberonbooks.com to read more about all our books and to buy them. You
will also find features, author interviews and news of any author events, and you can
sign up for e-newsletters so that you're always first to hear about our new releases.

Printed on FSC accredited paper

To Kate Howland

Cast

BEV, 48. A poet/academic.

TAMSIN, late 20s. Bev's PA.

DAVID, early 30s. A journalist.

MICHAEL, 22. An arts centre employee.

NOTES

/ denotes the point of interrupted speech.

Chana is pronounced with the 'ch' sound as in 'chutzpah'. Characters in the play might have their own interpretation.

ONE

Music, low volume – 'The Night' by Frankie Valli and the Four Seasons.

A room used as a study in North London. BEV sits at a desk you would expect a 48-year-old poet to own. There's a sofa downstage. A laptop is open but she's handwriting something she's not pleased with.

Bored, distracted, wanting to leave the task. Hums then sings, pours a large glass from a wine box and drinks it in a few glugs.

Goes to put the wine box away, change of mind, pours another large glass, drinks it straight down.

Turns music up.

She washes the glass up. Takes cigarettes out of the desk drawer, smokes out of the window. Takes a mint out of her pocket and puts it in her mouth.

She dances a bit.

Hears someone coming. Fans the air. Pretends to be working.

TAMSIN enters. Turns music off.

TAMSIN: terminado?

BEV: almost

TAMSIN: how almost?

    Sniffs the air, opens a window, starts tidying.

    smoking?

BEV: lapsed

TAMSIN: drinking?

BEV: no

TAMSIN: *(Shaking wine box.)* I've worked out why you've started buying these wine boxes

BEV: (?)

TAMSIN: you can't see the level going down…so I don't know how much you've had

BEV: next step vodka bottles stashed in the cistern

TAMSIN: *Bev*

when will it be ready?

BEV: blocked

TAMSIN: don't overthink it

Sorry is all you need.

BEV: what if I'm not sorry?

What if I didn't *do* anything?

TAMSIN: we're doing this, *really*? When we're this far?

You know what? I've, like, *had it*, if you…

go ahead, carry on like this

BEV: it's censorship is what it is

TAMSIN: like, fuck off Bev

BEV: is that how you talk to me Tamsin?

this is the *last* effing…

my dad *balanced*…

Silence.

TAMSIN: how is he?

BEV: Can you drive me later?

Why is it that hospices are so nice…gardens…make your own cups of tea…

I'm glad we went to Hastings… You remember what he said, when we were in the café?

TAMSIN: I dropped you, took me ages to park, remember?

BEV: I told you…my mum helped him with his *dark faults and cares* he said. They went away after he met her. Didn't ask what these *dark faults and cares* were…

might've been his language slipping with the dementia.

Beat.

What if I'm innocent? Don't *feel* guilty. If I was drunk, said something dodgy. It was *written down.* People read it, said nothing. You read it…

TAMSIN: I wasn't reading for that, I don't read for that.

Metre, assonance, symbolism…*that's* my job

BEV: it's like politics never happened to your generation

you even been on a demo?

TAMSIN: you know I have

BEV: when you were with that *anarchist*

What was his name?

TAMSIN: we had a plan

BEV: you agree I've done nothing?

TAMSIN: –

BEV: that this is just to make peace?

TAMSIN: it's like, gone back and forth in my mind /

BEV: oh fah-king hell! Not *perceptions* again?

TAMSIN: yes perceptions. Forms of words, juxtaposition of words…historic eggshells…shards of eggshells

BEV: poetry Tammy. We compare shit, it's our M.O.

TAMSIN: mmm, for an early morning walk on the beach maybe

You need to write that apology.

BEV: will it make you happy?

TAMSIN: make the world happy…back on its axis

BEV: Eighteen poems ignored, one picked at endlessly…

Not cos it's any good, not cos it speaks to people…

TAMSIN: please finish it

what have you got so far?

BEV walks to the table, sits, reads.

BEV: For the last thirty years I've been obsessed with the Israel/Palestine conflict /

TAMSIN: justifying

BEV: let me get into it

TAMSIN: first sentence should say *sorry*…not *you have to understand the context*…it's not for *me* to understand, it's for *you* to explain

BEV: oh-kay…

my enthusiasm for the cause of justice for the Palestinian people and my continuing support for the Boycott, Di / vest

TAMSIN: this sounds like sorry, not sorry

BEV: Boycott, Divestment and Sanctions movement

TAMSIN: no-one's even hearing you now

BEV: led me to overstep the mark /

TAMSIN: you like, slipped and fell into some anti-Semitism?

BEV: and write a few lines that are open to misinterpretation /

TAMSIN: open to?!

TAMSIN searches, finds volume and page.

here… *(reads)* 'she searches her bag like a nazi

did to her bubbe'

4

BEV: so?

TAMSIN: don't play with me Bev. You know as well as I do

Jew, nazi…nazi, Jew

Come on, don't pretend you don't understand

Those words can't be in the same room

BEV: You know bubbe is grandma?

TAMSIN: and now her soldier granddaughter's acting like a nazi?

BEV: do you not think she is?

TAMSIN: you'd say that of a Belgian soldier?

BEV: Yes! If Belgium had invaded part of France…

TAMSIN: *(Picking up the apology.)* it won't do

BEV: *(Looks at TAMSIN's screen.)* how's my Facebook page?

TAMSIN: they're still using upper case.

I'm changing your privacy settings.

BEV: Oh privacy! People are obsessed with it. Nothing to keep secret but their shopping preferences.

TAMSIN: any chance we can return to the point /

BEV: you don't think I'll get any of this…nastiness at tomorrow's gig?

TAMSIN: look, I know a journalist

BEV: –

TAMSIN: who'll interview you

BEV: sympathetically?

TAMSIN: he's good, also Jewish

BEV: bonus points…

TAMSIN: used to see my sister…

BEV: that's a recommendation?

TAMSIN: too many judgy judgements your honour

BEV: set it up…go on

TAMSIN: don't be like mad sexy bitch with him

BEV: (?)

TAMSIN: I was *in the room* when you offered oral sex to the man from *The Independent*

BEV: I didn't *mean* it

TAMSIN: you were drunk

> *Beat.*

BEV: some of us have to be…

TAMSIN: Jesus, not this again

BEV: *(Rhythmically.)* Dylan Thomas, Brendan Behan, Marguerite Duras, Dorothy Parker… Dylan Thomas, Jack Kerouak, Faulkner /

TAMSIN: think what they could've achieved without

BEV: think what they achieved *with*…

> *TAMSIN starts to open post. BEV goes back to the apology.*

BEV: are they all nasty?

TAMSIN: the support ones are worst…real-life Jew-baiters

BEV: it's a weird kind of hate

TAMSIN: *(Reads.)* ZIONISTS ARE RUNNING IT ALL YOU ARE DOUBLE RIGHT TO SAY THIS AND KEEP SAYING IT…THE SHEEPLE NEED TO OPEN THEIR EYES TO WHAT IS GOING ON AND WAKE UP!!! THE WORLD GOVERNMENT BANKER ROTHSCHILD BILDERBERG AND IT IS YOUR DUTY TO EXPOSE /

BEV: sheeple?

TAMSIN: it's a blend of sheep and people apparently...used by conspiracy theorists

BEV: for someone who *doesn't read for that,* you're very zeitgeisty

TAMSIN: you'd call it a steep learning curve

BEV: I like that...sheeple...where's he live?

TAMSIN: Torquay.

BEV: wonder what it is that the Jews run in Torquay?

A big deckchair cartel? Pedalo syndicate?

Beat.

TAMSIN: *(Waves letter.)* did you read this letter I left out for you, Mrs Marks from Stamford Hill, about her neighbour?

BEV: yes, terrible...

TAMSIN: *(Reads.)* a man in a tracksuit hit her hard on the side of the face and ran off. I found Mrs Levin in the street, on her hands and knees, trying to get up. Her nose was bleeding and she was trying not to cry.

Like, who the fuck would hit a seventy-three-year-old lady?

BEV: a fascist, clearly...they're scum

TAMSIN: she says you're not helping...things have got worse

BEV: he shouted the Polish word for Jew at her, you think it's likely he's inspired by a middle-aged lefty woman's poetry?

He's in an émigré nazi group

TAMSIN: she's not seeing the distinction, says your poem creates a climate

BEV: I did read it

TAMSIN: well?

7

BEV: it's fucking tragic and horrifying and so, so wrong...but Not. My. Fault. These fascists hate reds like they hate Jews.

First they came for the communists, remember?

I will write back though.

Beat.

TAMSIN: And this, this, ah

BEV: Tammy?

TAMSIN: student poetry society, Essex...you've been, like, *uninvited*

BEV: No Platformed?

TAMSIN: no...as such...'s polite...mentions *the current controversy*

BEV: the Dean's gonna *end* me next Wednesday. He hates me anyway.

I'll be ex-Visiting Professor. This will be fuel...

TAMSIN: Essex Poetry Soc won't do a press release

Holds letter up.

they write letters on Basildon Bond

Sniffs letter and looks curiously at it.

no-one will know about it

we'll get this interview to do a job for you

BEV: and he's ok this guy?

TAMSIN: David. More than

BEV: Tamsin?

TAMSIN: we've had coffees

BEV: coffees?

TAMSIN: for now

BEV: what did your sister say?

TAMSIN: story is she dumped him…work obsessed

BEV: *you'd* like that

TAMSIN: I wouldn't find it off-putting

BEV: Oh Tammy.

Offer him something special for a good review

TAMSIN: don't go off on one of your, like, riffs, answer the questions, turn yourself down a bit…try not to be so, so *Beverley* for an hour

BEV: riffs?

TAMSIN: umm… Facebook privacy perhaps? Why doner kebab is, like, the best food, no decent music since 1979, why there's no point to life outside the N7 postcode, people who drink red wine are sinister. And *all* politics

BEV: there'll be questions about politics

TAMSIN: which you will *listen* to and give measured answers. You will *not* say *Zionists*. If you wish to mention Israel, you're to talk about the current Israeli Government.

No make-up, be all contrite. After, you can, like, stand outside Holloway Road tube, drink a bottle of dirty rum and fight a passer-by…shag a passer-by even

BEV: ok, ok.

TAMSIN: I'm not doing this because we're friends /

BEV: we're friends?

TAMSIN: not everything's a joke…your work, your work which I *really* believe in, will suffer. I've been with you *six years* Bev. I'm not watching you fall apart, your *reputation* fall apart cos you can't *manage*…

BEV: six years is it?

TAMSIN: yeah, I'm doing it for the fucking money. Get me, I'm loaded

BEV: do I not pay you enough?

TAMSIN: durrr…you can't afford to, 'specially if you lose your job

BEV: that won't happen though?

TAMSIN: we must act fast, it's all about the *now*

BEV: it's only point two of a salary

TAMSIN: which amounts to *all* of my salary

> *Beat.*

did you read my poems?

BEV: I need proper time and space to do them justice

TAMSIN: you haven't read them and can't face me?

BEV: promise, this week

TAMSIN: I've not shown 'til now

BEV: that's why I want to give them real thoroughness

TAMSIN: they'll need work…be honest Bev

BEV: it's the only setting I have

> *Beat.*

For argument's sake, if the Dean was to fire me…how could I earn more money?

TAMSIN: drink less, work harder

BEV: if it were that simple

TAMSIN: it is. What about drinking every other day? I can get you work, bookshops, readings. We could go on tour again!

BEV: mmmm

TAMSIN: at least do some book reviews

BEV: god save me from dystopian novels...surely the world's shit enough without imagining a worse one

TAMSIN: you *never* followed up with that radio producer

BEV: god he got on my nerves

The world can do without my Oedipus Rex

TAMSIN: I'm going to say this now. Your energy levels and cognitive functions are, like, *impaired* /

BEV: WHAT?!

TAMSIN: you know it / are

BEV's phone rings, she points a finger at TAMSIN.

BEV: *(To caller.)* Yes, yes...is he?

I will, yes, yes...forty-five to an hour

Thanks

(To TAMSIN.) Dad...can you drive me?

TAMSIN: *(Nods.)*

BEV: this might be... I was going yesterday but what with...

TAMSIN: oh Bev

TAMSIN hugs BEV.

BEV: it's ok...they're not sure but...

They're leaving.

I'll catch you

Exit TAMSIN.

BEV sands in front of a framed photo of a man, 40ish. Touches it with her fingertips on the way out.

11

TWO

The night.

BEV is on her knees, staring at the photo, dressed for bed. She's compulsively scratching her left upper arm. TAMSIN, who was asleep on the sofa moves toward her and takes in the scene.

TAMSIN: Bev, come back

BEV stops scratching, looks at her arm.

BEV: come back?

come back to where?

TAMSIN gets on her knees and links her arms around BEV. Kisses the top of her head.

TAMSIN: come back

BEV turns her head toward TAMSIN.

Fade.

THREE

The following morning. The study.

BEV and TAMSIN asleep on the sofa under a blanket. Bottles everywhere. TAMSIN wakes hungover, extricates herself from sofa delicately. BEV snores a bit. TAMSIN starts to tidy and make coffee.

BEV: *(Talks in her sleep, inaudible.)*

TAMSIN stops to listen, then continues tidying. After a while BEV wakes.

paracetamol?

TAMSIN gets BEV paracetamol and water. Hands it to her.

TAMSIN starts working at her laptop.

What a night!

TAMSIN: I'll cancel David. The journalist. And the gig

BEV: don't

TAMSIN: no-one would expect

BEV: displacement activity

TAMSIN: let me cancel Bev…

BEV: no, I mean it

TAMSIN: hangover…your dad

BEV: he wouldn't approve of moping about. It's what he would've wanted, help with those *dark faults and cares*

TAMSIN: you can't…you're still drunk

BEV: when's he due?

TAMSIN: an hour

Seeing something shocking on laptop, reads it.

the Dean's written

BEV: oh

TAMSIN: in response…

BEV: response?

TAMSIN: to your email of…let's see…two forty-eight this morning

BEV: (?)

TAMSIN: oh yes Beverly

BEV: faaahk!

TAMSIN: *(Reads.)* that this constitutes gross misconduct… employment as Visiting Professor terminated with immediate effect…

BEV: can't have been *that* bad

TAMSIN: oh, it can

BEV: go on

TAMSIN: don't read it today. I'll explain your dad…

BEV: tell me

TAMSIN: starts off well, it's like, conciliatory, chatty…then it gets, like, bit *too* conciliatory

BEV: how can it be too conciliatory?

TAMSIN: the offer of a tittywank?

They laugh manically. BEV starts to cry quietly and TAMSIN comforts her.

you're sure about David? The gig?

BEV: bring it

TAMSIN: got the script?

BEV: the narrative is up here…remorse, empathy with the Chana character, no wish to offend…

TAMSIN: he's not out to set traps, he's not that sort. Don't do nervy rambling either…make him work

BEV: you'll be here, won't you?

TAMSIN: for most of it, I need to go on an errand

I'll be there in good time for the gig, those books won't sell themselves

Before you say it, they've got proper security…in case

Beat.

ok, practise… I'll be David

Beverley /

BEV: please, call me Bev

TAMSIN: Bev, tell me how you reacted when people said that your poem, Checkpoint Chana, was anti-Semitic?

BEV: horrified David. Never saw it coming.

TAMSIN: you didn't think 'she searches her bag like a nazi / did to her bubbe' would cause controversy?

BEV: I'm mortified David. I can't tell you.

No, I wanted to describe my empathy with the Chana character, she's based on a real person, a soldier I saw one day in Hebron

TAMSIN: it's written from an experience you had?

BEV: a trade union delegation a couple of years ago

TAMSIN: you're anti-Zionist?

BEV: is the wrong phrase for what I am. I'm a passionate believer in peace… I believe in two states

TAMSIN: ok, but you did know that comparing Israel to Nazi Germany is generally considered anti-Semitic

BEV: I certainly do now Dave!

TAMSIN: try, if I knew that it would be seen in that way I would never have

BEV: if I knew it would be seen in that way I would never have /

TAMSIN: it's not funny

BEV: not even bleakly?

TAMSIN: would you say you've learned from the experience?

BEV: I have. It's been a learning time, a journey if you like /

TAMSIN: if you're not /

BEV: I am…sorry…go on

TAMSIN: what would you say to Jewish people reading your poem who might be offended?

BEV: I'm so very sorry. Really. I've *never* been anti-Semitic… shall I say about the demo?

TAMSIN: without shoe-horning it in…if it feels natural

BEV: twenty-five years ago or so there was a series of incidents where Jewish cemeteries were desecrated and I went with friends from uni on the protest march

TAMSIN: Jewish friends?

BEV: one, I think. We were attacked by some local fascists…it was the worst, a boy was in hospital they beat him so badly

TAMSIN: that sounds terrible

BEV: I still think about it…so it just isn't in me to be…

TAMSIN: has the outcry changed you?

BEV: I need to challenge my assumptions… I'd like to revisit, listen to Israeli voices

TAMSIN: are you taking the piss?

BEV: I don't think I am…don't have to agree with those voices. We could go at Christmas, one of those bibley tours

TAMSIN: you can't afford it

BEV: *(Sings.) Oh little town of Bethlehem*

I'll do a national tour of Waterstones, how about that?

TAMSIN: if only you would

BEV: only don't ask me to go back to Chatham

TAMSIN: don't think they'll want you back

BEV: never had a crowd like it

TAMSIN: it wasn't you then?

BEV: funny bunch

TAMSIN: you won't have it, will you? You were off your face

BEV: I'd had ibuprofen for my knee

TAMSIN: you invited the *taxi driver* back to our hotel

BEV: you're just a snob…yep, I can feel a tour coming on, you know I always have a creative upsurge on tour

TAMSIN: only upsurge I've seen is all the vomiting…still, liking where your head's at…positive

BEV: maybe Dad going will be a catalyst, like when Thomas Hardy's wife died

(Quotes Hardy.) So I went on softly from the glade,
And left her behind me throwing her shade,
As she were indeed an apparition –
My head unturned lest my dream should fade.

TAMSIN: *(Acknowledges the quote.)* you'll need help, the funeral

BEV: please

Brief silence.

BEV: he liked you

TAMSIN: I only met him twice

17

BEV: always on about you…thought you were my daughter towards the end…I had to tell him that we were more like sisters

TAMSIN: –

BEV: and I'm the younger one, who needs help…

TAMSIN: do that apology now, I'll email the Dean

They both sit down to write.

BEV: loved cowboy films

TAMSIN: –

BEV: when I was a teenager I'd argue with him about Native Americans…over his head

you're too young but…every Saturday night on TV in the seventies… He loved *Shane*, watched it over and over when they got a video

TAMSIN: who's in that?

BEV: Alan Ladd, Jean Arthur. Unusual in its day cos Arthur is the romantic lead and she's fifty-three

TAMSIN: unusual now

BEV: wonder what his *dark faults and cares* were?

Beat.

talk to me again about TV work, come on

TAMSIN: you're joking

BEV: I'm really not

TAMSIN: you said

BEV: new era

TAMSIN: it would mean money, you could put a book out at Christmas

BEV: a tie in?

TAMSIN: you could *actually* do this, women academics all over TV now…talk about raising your profile…you'd be seriously fantastic Bev!

BEV: not too old?

TAMSIN: we'd need to look at outfits…maybe botox, collagen, I have a friend

BEV: I won't end up with a trout pout?

TAMSIN: she's all about subtle. I am so like, *fucking* excited about this!

BEV: you really think

TAMSIN: you're used to lectures, readings, projecting yourself

You're sure about tonight?

BEV: if I'd cancelled readings every time I'd had a few drinks…

TAMSIN: and you know what you're gonna do?

BEV: well, I thought I'd start with Chana

TAMSIN: don't even!

Listen, the next few days is like, a *pivotal* time for us

BEV: us?

TAMSIN: yes, *us*

We have to make sure that we make the right choices.

If we do, we're ok and you'll have a career, be someone who is employable and commissionable. If your name comes up at a Tufnell Park dinner party, it's ok for people to say they like you

It's like, the time when people say, *what d'you think prime minister, shall we go to war?*…or that time when your best friend's boyfriend (who you've always secretly liked) puts his hand on your upper thigh…

Get it wrong and it's, like, all over. One outburst, one show of temper…

There's one thing I want an answer to first…

Beat.

BEV: you want to know if I'm anti-Semitic

Beat.

Never was, never can be

Beat.

TAMSIN studies her carefully and nods.

Look, phase one of being a TV star is rehabilitation. The telly doesn't want a stinking anti-Semite, get ready, shower, now!

TAMSIN ushers BEV offstage. She watches her down the hall. Finds her phone and dials, looks behind her as she waits for an answer.

Fade.

FOUR

BEV's flat. BEV is alone in the study, pretending to read. We see TAMSIN and DAVID in the hall.

DAVID: is it still ok to do the interview?

TAMSIN: *(Nods.)* She's in a bit of a state

DAVID: you're gonna leave soon?

TAMSIN: she doesn't know where I'm going. Don't tell her if she asks.

How was your cricket practice?

DAVID: Good. I say good but I'm having trouble working the ball off my legs

TAMSIN: is that bad?

DAVID: it's a bread and butter shot, I'm lost without it.

Are we still going out tonight?

TAMSIN: god yes! I'll need a break from her by then.

That sounds bad, doesn't it, with her dad

DAVID: you're very patient with her

TAMSIN: Look, someone sent a letter, very vague, saying there might be a protest tonight, I hid it from her

DAVID: shit! She won't like that

TAMSIN: I can't tell her

DAVID: don't

TAMSIN: what if it happens though, she'll freak

DAVID: people write these things, rarely actually happen

He puts his hands on her waist.

TAMSIN: that's interesting

DAVID: it's one of my best moves

TAMSIN: they say that, do they?

She kisses him and pushes him away.

They enter the study.

TAMSIN: This is David Bev

BEV: good to meet you David

DAVID: and you Beverley...

BEV: Bev, please

DAVID: I'm so sorry, your dad

BEV: that's kind of you

DAVID: I'm not trying to catch you out today, you're safe...
I want you to know...

TAMSIN: and you don't have to convert him cos he's a fan

BEV: ah, to be interviewed by a prepared hack

DAVID: I've brought a book if you don't /

BEV: please, yes...

DAVID goes into his bag and pulls out the volume, passes it to BEV, who signs it.

BEV: I'll make it to you?

DAVID: yes, thanks

BEV: are you a conventional David, no 'e' in the middle or anything?

DAVID: I'm a conventional David...

BEV: what did you think?

DAVID: in terms of the poetry, great...

BEV: but

DAVID: it's the but I'm here to talk about

BEV: it's been a brutal time, hasn't it Tammy?

TAMSIN: the last thing we /

BEV: the last thing

DAVID takes a recorder out of his pocket, shows it to BEV and she nods.

DAVID: so… I'm here to get your side. I realise you're not a politician but you seem to have wandered into that area?

BEV: I've always been political but never brought much of that to the work. The poem was meant as reportage, an observation…

DAVID: but with those unfortunate comparisons

BEV: the nazi thing

DAVID: there's also a mention of apartheid

BEV: yes

DAVID: and you regret that too?

BEV: wasn't it the nazi simile getting all the attention?

DAVID: apartheid will stir up feelings too

BEV: I've new vistas since the start of the…*controversy*

DAVID: and I want to bring that across. I'm not trying to turn you over Bev

BEV: I'm grateful to you

DAVID: it's a great gig for me too

BEV: let me read you an apology we've put on Facebook

DAVID: ok!

BEV: *(Reads.)* The first thing to say is sorry. Sorry for the offence caused by my poem, Checkpoint Chana. It won't appear in future editions of the volume.

From the response to the poem and the way that I have been rightly taken to ask, I now understand how wrong it is to suggest any link between Israel and the Nazis. I also now understand how hurtful this might be.

I've always considered myself to be free of anti-Semitism and all forms of racism and my initial reaction is that I was not guilty. However, having read about and discussed with many people what constitutes anti-Semitic language, I feel I need to apologise and learn a lesson. Again, I am deeply sorry.

DAVID: no-one could ask for more

BEV: mortified David, I really am

DAVID: would you say you've learned from the experience

BEV: so much…if I'd have known that it might be seen as an attack on Jewish people…

DAVID: for what it's worth, I think you've been a bit badly treated in all this

BEV: (?)

DAVID: thought the poem was great, crossed a line maybe but up with your best

I feel we're empathising with the Chana character. Her meanness comes from being in a place that neither her, nor the Arab woman, want to be at…

BEV: you read me well

TAMSIN: still, however good in the literary sense, there are more important issues. We realise that now

BEV: yes, we do

TAMSIN: I'm gonna have to go

BEV: you did say…what was it?

TAMSIN: an errand…family

BEV: oh-*kay*...tonight then, early

> *TAMSIN exits.*

BEV: I need to ask you about your intentions toward my employee

DAVID: (?)

BEV: *jokes*

DAVID: yes, I /

BEV: didn't mean to embarrass

DAVID: took me by surprise

BEV: ditto apartheid. Clever.

> drink?

DAVID: ummm...ok

BEV: white wine

DAVID: is good

BEV: you'll be kind to me, won't you?

DAVID: you'll be happy with it

BEV: you know where she's gone?

DAVID: (?)

> *BEV hands DAVID a large glass of wine.*

DAVID: are you working on anything?

BEV: spending a fortnight at a shack on the Kent coast soon. I'm sticking with beaches and nature from now on.

> Fifty shades of kelp

DAVID: the travel worked for you artistically

> Not been to Israel for ten years, very evocative what you did

BEV: that's kind. It's a weird place isn't it?

DAVID: yep

BEV: didn't know what to expect…memories from school. Musty bibles with scary pictures…biblical epics

DAVID: spent a summer there when I was seventeen. Odd being in the majority…kibbutz on the Dead Sea coast. Avocado picking…

BEV: I really wanted that experience, I *knew* it would spark something off.

Beat.

I knew when I saw her, the Chana girl, that there was a poem there. She looked so young, so hot, so *bored*…all that hair. Seemed like everything was an effort…like she was depressed

when's your next coffee with my PA?

DAVID: dinner, tonight, after your reading

BEV's already finished her wine, goes to fill up. Offers DAVID who declines.

BEV: you're coming?

DAVID: thought it would help with the piece

BEV: she'll be fit for work in the morning?

DAVID: we won't be out late

BEV: where will you go?

DAVID: new place… Shoreditch

BEV: –

DAVID: a modern twist on the Wimpey Bar

BEV: Christ in a fucking sandwich!

DAVID: mental eh?

BEV: last days of the Roman Empire…

DAVID: Late Capitalism…you have to walk through a florist to get to it

BEV: modern twist?

DAVID: shovelled on irony. Ethically locally sourced burgers

BEV: locally sourced in *Shoreditch*?

Beat.

DAVID: did you read her work? I'm biased, but I liked it…

BEV: I've never been good at this…a friend's poetry

DAVID: you didn't?

BEV: I *really* didn't. Hoping that she'll forget

DAVID: she won't. She's non-stop

BEV: have to face it

DAVID: you didn't see *anything* in them?

BEV: not a fucking thing. The work of a person who can't let go. She's very anal, top quality in a PA, rubbish for a poet

Listen, I love Tammy but poems aren't her thing. I wonder if she wouldn't be a novelist, she's got patience, work ethic

DAVID: oh…

BEV: she tell you I'm gonna be a TV star?

DAVID: said she's always trying to talk to you/

BEV: do you think I'll be any good?

DAVID: you'd be super

BEV: why d'you say that?

DAVID: you're authentic

BEV: try another word…authentic sounds like I'm wearing a fleece covered in cat hair, delivering anti-fracking leaflets

DAVID: how about arty milf?

BEV: I'll take that thank you. Silf is more correct though

DAVID: (?)

BEV: spinster I'd like to…

DAVID: Is that a picture of your dad?

BEV: dear Dad

BEV fills her glass, he declines. She gestures to the tape recorder, he switches it off.

DAVID: no, that's fine. What was he like?

BEV: get on with it, don't ask questions type. Taught P.E. for thirty years. Nice man but how would you say, he didn't value diversity. Very good with fruit trees, had *dark faults and cares* when he was young apparently

DAVID: ah

BEV: arty milf eh? I like that… Tammy wants me to have botox

DAVID: a lot of people do now

BEV: I'll consult my principles on this

DAVID: any offers yet?

BEV: dreaming of location work in Greece. Bullshitting on Sophocles, gently sweating under a linen dress

DAVID: I like it

Beat.

BEV: you know where she's gone?

DAVID: (?)

BEV: she's a bad liar, wouldn't go unless it was vital. Can't see her trusting me with you

DAVID: oh?

BEV: she'd worry I'd be off message. Fuck it up by saying Jews have horns and control the media

DAVID: why would she think that?

BEV: you might have noticed, I'm a bit of a pisshead. I say things I don't mean.

It's something I'm working on

Beat.

DAVID: like I say, you're safe

BEV: you know don't you

Tammy, what she's doing

DAVID: no…let's move on. The Kent coast you / say

BEV: tell me David

DAVID: –

BEV: seriously now, *tell me*

DAVID: she cares about you

BEV: she's up to something

I'll get it out of her

DAVID: you need to let her help you

BEV: why does everyone think I need help all the time?

DAVID: –

BEV: you *can* say it

DAVID: you've made no secret of your mental health issues over the years, it's to your credit

BEV: I saw an artistic gap in the market…suicide verse

DAVID: you've moved on

BEV: I'm still Bev the nutter though. That's what you all think

DAVID: your early work is very important

BEV: and my later stuff isn't?

DAVID: don't straw man me Bev

BEV: how d'you think it feels knowing that your best work was done nearly thirty years ago?

DAVID: I'd be glad if I have something to look back on

Not everybody has that Bev

DAVID prepares to leave.

I'll see you tonight then

BEV: so, you've enough to be getting on with?

DAVID: you'll be fine, my piece will be ok. I've met anti-Semites and you're not one. You pass the sniff test.

DAVID and BEV exchange a look.

Fade.

FIVE

A studio theatre in North London.

MICHAEL is in the tech booth offstage. Lectern downstage right. Table upstage has glasses and bottles of wine. A bright white light shines on BEV who briefly holds a crucifixion pose.

BEV: *(Testing acoustics.)* Your frowsty coat
    Made in Yugoslavia
    Aramis, Bensons, sweat; ripped lining.
    In King's Cross and the midnight cinemas
    open and we get Montgomery Clift

MICHAEL: that's cold

BEV: a warm wash?

    my PA should *be here* by now

    The light changes to an orange tone.

    That's the lady poet's light….Michael is it?

MICHAEL: Yes, Michael

    you move about much?

BEV: I'm poetry, not spoken word. Page not stage.

    A few steps. Stops pins and needles

MICHAEL: No specials?

BEV: –

MICHAEL: you want a mic? Got a clip-on if you want it?

BEV: the sound is *nice*…like a church harvest festival

    MICHAEL makes his way to the stage. Preparing by moving chairs, pouring multiple glasses of wine. BEV stands at the lectern arranges papers, scoring volumes with pencil. Drinks from a large glass of wine.

BEV: bit of a whiff in here. Bodies. Like a gym.

MICHAEL: dance class. Mixed ability Lindy Hop

> *Beat.*

> my mum's a fan

BEV: aged 45 to 60 with an arts degree?

MICHAEL: she likes to recite your famous one. The one you started then

BEV: these her books?

MICHAEL: would you mind?

BEV: what's her name?

MICHAEL: Hattie. Like Hattie Jacques she says. She's fed up she can't come

BEV: give me your phone

MICHAEL: (?)

BEV: I'll record a video message for her, she'll like that

> *MICHAEL gives BEV his phone showing her how to record.*

BEV: (*Recording on phone cheek to cheek with MICHAEL.*) Hi Hattie, Bev Hemmings here, I'm with Michael. He's a lovely boy, you must be proud.

> Shame you can't make it tonight, I need all the fans I can get at the moment. Take care, Byyee!

> *BEV gives MICHAEL the phone.*

MICHAEL: she won't believe this

BEV: don't tell anyone. I cannot have it getting about that I'm not queen bitch

> *She starts to sign half a dozen volumes on the table.*

MICHAEL: few more lines? Just to check sound

> *MICHAEL moves into audience.*

BEV: A fresh knife
  Kept in our room, points down
  His bleak, failed bed
  Broken half-light in a Le Corbusier half-dream

MICHAEL: What's it about?

BEV: student life…council flats…infidelity…

MICHAEL: you the victim?

BEV: that's me in the picture wearing the horns

MICHAEL: sorry

BEV: –

MICHAEL: for bringing it up

BEV: twenty-three published poems on the subject. I'm officially over it…

  You like it here, your job?

MICHAEL: all eighteen hours a week of it

BEV: you've got other work?

MICHAEL: overnight Saturday, Sunday in Tesco's

BEV: oh

MICHAEL: you don't like to turn it down.

  I've got a HNC in Stage Management…

BEV: but it's not /

MICHAEL: I'm living at home

  Beat.

BEV: Can you look in the bar, see If my PA's out there?…

  MICHAEL starts to leave, stops, turns.

MICHAEL: How will I?

BEV: late twenties, knitted beret…mouth set like a cat's arse

She pulls a disapproving face, imitating TAMSIN.

MICHAEL exits. BEV messes with her hair. Stands, hands on hips looking at an imaginary audience.

With no extension beyond
How we were in January
Icy Heath and Keats' House
Waterlow Park, the cemetery

Where *is* she? Am I expected to take the money myself? Introduce myself?

BEV punches herself hard to the forehead.

She walks to the table and downs two glasses of wine, refills them.

MICHAEL enters, seeing the glass refilling only.

MICHAEL: no PA I could see…not many men.

BEV: my crowd look like librarians with a Revlon addiction

MICHAEL: some are smoking by the doors

BEV: any of them look demonstratey? Placards aloft?

MICHAEL: mum *said* you were being called anti-Jewish. You're not are you?

BEV: no, do I look like?

MICHAEL: what do they look like?

BEV: not like me

my PA said she'd be here for now, not like her to be late

BEV walks to the table, picks up a glass and drinks…

MICHAEL: *(Indicates the glasses.)* not for me to say but…

BEV: you're in safe hands…take a lot more than *that*

MICHAEL: I'd be on the floor by now

BEV: *(Looks at him carefully.)* yes, you probably would

MICHAEL: not my thing

BEV: it's very much my thing

MICHAEL: you alright?

BEV: my dad died yesterday

MICHAEL: should you be here?

BEV: I make a point of doing what people warn me against.

Where the fuck is she?

Look, if it comes to it, would you introduce me?

MICHAEL: I wouldn't know... Oh...go on... I'll give it a try, why not? What's the worst?

BEV: 's easy... I'll write it down

MICHAEL: I'm a bit informal

BEV: won't matter, let me write it down, then we can work on it

BEV starts to write a script.

MICHAEL's phone rings, he answers.

MICHAEL: Yes Mum...

Yes it is exciting...

Yeah, very nice...

No, not at all like that...

I'll tell her...

No, I said, I can't

Mum, I'm not going to Jade's baby's christening

Because we're not that close, I've not seen her in over ten years

No! Sorry but no

It's not about a suit, I don't want you to buy me a suit

No, not even for interviews, I don't go to those sort of interviews

I'm sorry you feel like that

About eleven, eleven thirty

Yeah bye

(To BEV.) she says thanks

BEV: I wish I had someone who bought me clothes

MICHAEL: It's too much. I love her but I'm *twenty-two*

Beat.

Blackout.

MICHAEL: don't worry, probably easily fixed

MICHAEL moves back to the tech booth.

BEV: oh, for fuck's sake!

Well, this is shit for arseholes!

MICHAEL: won't be a big problem... I don't expect

BEV: what if it is *a big problem*!?

MICHAEL: what will be...

BEV: don't give me that Zen shit, George fucking Harrison

Beat.

MICHAEL: keep calm Bev

BEV: fucking hell!

How long's it gonna take?

Are you old enough to be doing this?

Beat.

MICHAEL: it's either gonna be something I can do straight away or we'll have to call the electrician we use. I shouldn't really even be doing this…

BEV: where is that that useless bitch?!

MICHAEL: oh*kaya*…worse things happen… I think we are…

Lights on. TAMSIN is present.

BEV: –

TAMSIN: the useless bitch is here

TAMSIN and BEV face each other.

Fade.

SIX

Arts Centre, 20 minutes later. The reading.

TAMSIN: Hi. It's lovely to see so many people here tonight. Before Bev comes on I'll share tonight's programme.

Right, ok, straight after me Bev will read for around 45 minutes and, like, talk through the background to the writing of the poems. She won't take questions from the floor but will be happy to chat at the signing which'll start about five minutes after we finish.

So, Bev…where to start? Winner at the age of twenty-one of a series of prizes for her first collection, *The Flat Above Star Food and Wine*, she's a place in the hearts of many for her fearless description of her mental health issues at that time.

A host of awards and prizes followed for further volumes, among them, *The Water is Only Three Feet Deep* and *Car Park Fight Operetta*.

She's been described in many ways, her favourite, she tells me, is from the New Musical Express, who referred to her in a 1989 review as, *a Sylvia Plath for the Morrissey generation.*

She'll also be reading tonight from her new collection, *The Olive Oil Lamp*. Please welcome Beverley Hemmings…

Applause.

BEV enters and takes her place at the lectern. She has a large glass of wine. She drinks, toasts the crowd.

TAMSIN takes a seat upstage left, quite close to Bev.

BEV: Hello Camden Town!

I hear Camden is the poetry capital of England

I've had a bit of a time of it in the last couple of weeks. Public and private stuff.

You might have read about me and a particular poem. In the papers. I'm anti-Semitic apparently. Bev the Jew-hater.

But that isn't my story. People are saying *all* criticism of Israel is anti-Semitic. You're not *allowed* to speak out. They've put land mines round the subject…if you touch it a shit bomb explodes over you, and no-one listens to the woman covered in shit

I'm under heavy manners

Look, I don't believe Jews are in a big conspiracy…

Don't believe any of the *tropes*…

If you're an artist you have to take risks they say. That's what they tell you…until you take a risk…

So here it is, *that* poem, 'Checkpoint Chana'

Beat.

our day trip guide is Jamal
of the hollow eyes.
The Judean mountains

She coughs.

Excuse me…
The Judean mountains
where elephants lived and the
patriarchs/matriarchs buried
Sarah, Abraham, Rebecca, Leah, Isaac and Jacob
the Cave of the Patriarchs
both Mosque and Synagogue
has an apartheid road
and bullet-proof glass

BEV watches a few people leave. Flaps a hand to hurry them.

Off you go then…quickly quickly…you're ruining it…

'That side's for Jews
That's for Arabs.'
Later I see her
in Hebron
a gate between district H1 and H2
slim dusty street blocked
cabin above, stairs up to it
turnstile at street level
Hillsborough cages
and she's all like
green beret, low-slung M16
pre-Raph gold hair
tied back with a black band
'Move! Move!'
Chana orders
in bored urgency
checking passes
the woman presents
she searches her bag
like a nazi did to her bubbe
Chana's hot and Chana's tired
grit in her eyes
in need of an *ice cold coke*
on the back of her throat
wet/dry
dry/wet
sweat stains under her arms
like contours on the map.
She would rather be
would rather be…

BEV watches a few more people leave and shrugs.

Fade.

SEVEN

*Arts Centre. BEV, TAMSIN and DAVID. Tables are set up for the signing.
They're watching the last audience members/staff leave. BEV waves to the
stragglers. Row starts immediately they see the door shut.*

BEV: I know, I know!

Went well otherwise though. Plenty of books Tammy

TAMSIN: you've, like, fucked it all up again. I carefully *unfucked*
it, now you've re-fucked it.

All we talked about...*preparation*...cos you can't cope with
me being late

BEV: don't be like it. Mistake, won't happen again

TAMSIN: no...that's it now, it's over

BEV: don't be stupid Tammy

DAVID: there were *other* press here

BEV: really? I didn't see /

DAVID: Standard, Guardian, Jewish Chronicle /

BEV: balls to the Jewish Chronicle! Fuck their shit!

DAVID: their Jewish shit?

BEV: Let's play spot the red anti-Semite. A game for one or
more careful players. Rule one, all lefties are Jew-haters...

You ever meet a Jew who's been chased by a gang of
Trotskyists? Jumped by a bunch of Corbynistas?

The black hundreds...nazis... the fash...they're the ones
who want to put you in a camp...did you not listen in
school?

DAVID: camps is it? Don't hold back

DAVID nods, gestures for BEV to take it up a notch.

BEV: you understand eff all…you deliberately misunderstand…
most people don't even know you're a Jew

DAVID: you'd be surprised

BEV: all those hours talking racism with your black friends at
the paper… What?! *None* of your colleagues are black?! I
find that astounding…what forces could be at work?!

DAVID: there are actually, at the paper, a few black colleagues /

BEV: not tucked away in admin, HR. I mean journalists, black
people with names like Clarke and Thompson…

That's what racism is David Gluckstein, the denial of *jobs*
and *life chances*, not a fucking poem that *offends* you!

Look, I don't deny some terrible things happen, *(to
TAMSIN)* the lady who was attacked in Stamford Hill…
but for most people in this country anti-Semitism is
homeopathic racism, a trace, a memory…it's been diluted
to virtual non-existence…

Compare your life to the people I met in West Bank
refugee camps…compare *your* life in London to a Bethnal
Green Bengali…

TAMSIN: Bev! Shut up!

BEV: I'm tired of it Tammy and I'm calling it out. He's
probably never taken a step out of NW3. What did the
people do to you David? Did your CV once get passed
over cos of your surname?

DAVID: you know nothing

TAMSIN: you really need to SHUT UP!

BEV: *(To TAMSIN, pointing.)* I've had it with you, you're holding
me back

TAMSIN: I'm holding *you* back! Six *years* of your fucking world.

Why does every-fucking-thing have to be about *you*?

Acting as an unpaid carer. Putting you on the toilet at night like a child, checking you've not left fags burning. Encouraging you to get out of bed when you're full of sweaty remorse…

Throwing out your men in the morning while you hide in the bathroom

Driving you…even to your dad's care home cos you're too lazy to get on a tube /

BEV: you know I have panic attacks on escalators

TAMSIN: I would if I drank as much as you

Your work is shit now Beverley, everyone says. Remember that review, '*nothing of consequence in this century.*'

BEV: *my* work is shit! That's good from someone who thinks being fat shamed in Topshop as a teenager is a subject for poetry!

TAMSIN: IT WAS NEW LOOK…you fucking bitch!

Brief silence. BEV and TAMSIN face off.

So you had read them. Thanks for your opinion. Understand where we are now

DAVID: you'd be on the 134 home from school and the boys who get on at Kentish Town would sit behind you and go *(hissing sound)* sssssssss…the sound of gas.

Type of shit still goes on my nephew says…

Beat.

This boy, he's only seven and he's out with his grandma. It's a bright day in winter and they're going for Haribos but first they go and see grandad at the cemetery. They go every time he spends the day with her. The boy has a flat brown oval pebble ready to put on the grave.

They're never sad in the cemetery because grandad wouldn't have liked it. He wasn't happy if you weren't happy grandma says.

They turn the last corner and it's all different. Beer cans, spray paint...

Some of the stones are broken and pushed over. Some have the symbol on them. Others have a one and an eight written on them.

Grandad's headstone has a sky blue swastika on it. Grandma goes to bend down but then she turns and ushers the boy away. She's crying. The boy wants to help tidy up and put the stones back up but grandma says they'll tell people and they will sort it. She's talking to herself. The boy wants to comfort her but doesn't know what to say.

He needs to know more about the people that did this. He can't sleep for thinking about it. His friend tells him that the one and eight mean Hitler's initials, their place in the alphabet...

The boy keeps the pebble with him forever...

DAVID takes out his wallet and removes the pebble, kisses it from habit and holds it up shoulder high.

TAMSIN and BEV go to DAVID. BEV kisses him on the cheek. DAVID touches her arm.

DAVID is avoiding tears, holds his hand up in farewell and exits.

TAMSIN follows DAVID out.

BEV is alone. She begins to collect her books, puts them in her bag. MICHAEL enters.

MICHAEL: you did the poem then

BEV: yes

MICHAEL: I could hear arguing

BEV: it was me doing the poem that caused the argument

MICHAEL: ah. Thought so

BEV: and?

MICHAEL: not really anything

BEV: no, go on. I'm taking advice today. Let's have it

MICHAEL: Mum rang again

BEV: what'd she say?

MICHAEL: two things, one, I don't need to go to the christening…

BEV: and two?

MICHAEL: she said if I get a chance to talk to you before the reading, ask you please not to do the poem, it's not more important than you she said

BEV: good advice. She's right, tell her

MICHAEL: we'd be fine if I could move out, see her and dad once a week

BEV: I moved out when I was eighteen, people did then. Only ever went back for a couple of months

MICHAEL: was that when you were ill?

BEV: she told you about that?

MICHAEL: I've just been reading one of your books

BEV: like it?

MICHAEL: I think so…not sure if I understand it all

BEV: don't think you are meant to *understand* poetry. It's not like geography. I don't understand parts of what I write and I've written it

MICHAEL: please take care of yourself

BEV: I will. You locking up?

MICHAEL: five minutes... I'll be back

MICHAEL smiles, BEV returns the smile.

MICHAEL exits.

TAMSIN re-enters.

BEV: you've got a new job then

TAMSIN: how did you know?

BEV: the way you've been. The way you upped and left yesterday. People don't look like you did when they're running an errand. You're not exactly the ice-cold *playa* type Tammy

Who's it with?

TAMSIN: your publisher

BEV: they know top class

TAMSIN: you'll be ok

BEV: been trying to grasp OK hard by the wrists and dance with him for thirty-five years

TAMSIN: I mean you'll cope

BEV: who'll be the new Tammy?

TAMSIN: you don't need a new Tammy. A new PA would be best...

A *working* relationship

BEV: will *we* be friends? Do friend things?

TAMSIN: d'you want that?

BEV: what about the pictures? I've not been in ages

TAMSIN: can it just be what's on that week though? Not *researched*

BEV smiles.

TAMSIN smiles, they hug.

TAMSIN: you hate my poems

BEV: we'll work on them...together

TAMSIN: they're no good, aren't they?

BEV: I see what you're trying to say... I'll help with that...

I was angry before...there's an essence worth polishing...
When I started I had help...editing, *opinions*...you need the
same as I had. Be fine...

Am I finished?

TAMSIN: I'll manage it. Allude to a mental health crisis...if
that's...?

BEV: don't see why being a nutter shouldn't work to my
advantage

Beat.

BEV: remember that hat you used to wear

TAMSIN: (?)

BEV: wool, quite jazzy, dark pinks and greens...tam o' shanter

TAMSIN: oh, yes

BEV: I liked it

TAMSIN: you can have it

BEV: I liked the way you looked in it....

Beat.

TAMSIN: I'll help you with those dark faults and cares

Beat.

I'm gonna try and... David...if you're ok to...?

BEV: I'll be alright...go!

TAMSIN exits.

BEV is alone, close to tears.

She scatches her left upper arm.

(Whispers.) I'm sorry

Fade.

The End.